PAUL ROMANUK

HOCKEY
SUPERSTARS

2013-2014

Your complete guide to the 2013–2014 season,
featuring action photos of
your favorite players

SCHOLASTIC
TORONTO NEW YORK LONDON AUCKLAND SYDNEY
MEXICO CITY NEW DELHI HONG KONG BUENOS AIRES

THE TEAMS

ANAHEIM DUCKS
team colors: purple, green, silver and white
home arena: Honda Center
mascot: Wild Wing
Stanley Cups won: 1

. . . .

CALGARY FLAMES
team colors: red, gold, black and white
home arena: Scotiabank Saddledome
mascot: Harvey the Hound
Stanley Cups won: 1

. . . .

EDMONTON OILERS
team colors: white, navy blue, orange and red
home arena: Rexall Place
Stanley Cups won: 5

LOS ANGELES KINGS
team colors: purple, white, black and silver
home arena: Staples Center
mascot: Bailey
Stanley Cups won: 2

. . . .

PHOENIX COYOTES
team colors: red, green, sand, sienna and purple
home arena: Jobing.com Arena
mascot: Howler

SAN JOSE SHARKS
team colors: teal, gray, orange and black
home arena: HP Pavilion at San Jose
mascot: S.J. Sharkie

. . . .

VANCOUVER CANUCKS
team colors: blue, silver, green and white
home arena: Rogers Arena
mascot: Fin

BOSTON BRUINS
nickname: Bs
team colors: gold, black and white
home arena: TD Garden
mascot: Blades the Bruin
Stanley Cups won: 6

. . . .

BUFFALO SABRES
team colors: black, white, red, gray and silver
home arena: First Niagara Center
mascot: Sabretooth

. . . .

OTTAWA SENATORS
nickname: Sens
team colors: black, red and gold
home arena: Canadian Tire Centre
mascot: Spartacat
Stanley Cups won:
7 (pre-1934 team)

TAMPA BAY LIGHTNING
nickname: Bolts
team colors: blue, black, silver and white
home arena: Tampa Bay Times Forum
mascot: ThunderBug
Stanley Cups won: 1

. . . .

TORONTO MAPLE LEAFS
nickname: Leafs
team colors: blue and white
home arena: Air Canada Centre
mascot: Carlton the Bear
Stanley Cups won: 11

DETROIT RED WINGS
nickname: Wings
team colors: red and white
home arena: Joe Louis Arena
mascot (unofficial): Al the octopus
Stanley Cups won: 11

. . . .

MONTREAL CANADIENS
nickname: Habs
team colors: red, blue and white
home arena: Bell Centre
mascot: Youppi
Stanley Cups won: 24

. . . .

FLORIDA PANTHERS
nickname: Cats
team colors: red, navy blue, yellow and gold
home arena: BB&T Center
mascot: Stanley C. Panther

WESTERN CONFERENCE – CENTRAL DIVISION

CHICAGO BLACKHAWKS
nickname: Hawks
team colors: red, black and white
home arena: United Center
mascot: Tommy Hawk
Stanley Cups won: 5

COLORADO AVALANCHE
nickname: Avs
team colors: burgundy, silver, black and blue
home arena: Pepsi Center
mascot: Bernie
Stanley Cups won: 2

DALLAS STARS
team colors: green, white, black and gold
home arena: American Airlines Center
Stanley Cups won: 1

NASHVILLE PREDATORS
nickname: Preds
team colors: navy blue, silver, white and gold
home arena: Bridgestone Arena
mascot: Gnash

MINNESOTA WILD
team colors: red, green, gold and wheat
home arena: Xcel Energy Center
mascot: Nordy

WINNIPEG JETS
team colors: blue, silver, red and white
home arena: MTS Centre
mascot: Mick E. Moose

ST. LOUIS BLUES
team colors: white, navy blue and gold
home arena: Scottrade Center
mascot: Louie

EASTERN CONFERENCE – METROPOLITAN DIVISION

CAROLINA HURRICANES
nickname: Canes
team colors: red, black and white
home arena: PNC Arena
mascot: Stormy
Stanley Cups won: 1

COLUMBUS BLUE JACKETS
nickname: Jackets
team colors: blue, red and green
home arena: Nationwide Arena
mascot: Stinger

NEW YORK RANGERS
nickname: Blueshirts
team colors: blue, white and red
home arena: Madison Square Garden
Stanley Cups won: 4

NEW YORK ISLANDERS
nickname: Isles
team colors: orange, blue, white, silver and green
home arena: Nassau Veterans Memorial Coliseum
mascot: Sparky the Dragon
Stanley Cups won: 4

PITTSBURGH PENGUINS
nickname: Pens
team colors: black, gold and white
home arena: Consol Energy Center
mascot: Iceburgh
Stanley Cups won: 3

PHILADELPHIA FLYERS
team colors: orange, white and black
home arena: Wells Fargo Center
Stanley Cups won: 2

NEW JERSEY DEVILS
team colors: red, black and white
home arena: Prudential Center
mascot: N.J. Devil
Stanley Cups won: 3

WASHINGTON CAPITALS
nickname: Caps
team colors: blue, black, gold and white
home arena: Verizon Center
mascot: Slapshot

YOUR FAVORITE TEAM

Name of your favorite team: _____

Conference and division: _____

Players on your favorite team at the start of the season:

Number	Name	Position
_____	_____	_____
_____	_____	_____
_____	_____	_____
_____	_____	_____
_____	_____	_____
_____	_____	_____
_____	_____	_____
_____	_____	_____
_____	_____	_____
_____	_____	_____
_____	_____	_____
_____	_____	_____
_____	_____	_____
_____	_____	_____

Changes, Trades, New Players

_____   _____   _____
_____   _____   _____
_____   _____   _____
_____   _____   _____
_____   _____   _____
_____   _____   _____
_____   _____   _____

End-of-Season Standings

Fill in the name of the team you think will finish in first place in each of the four NHL Divisions.

WESTERN CONFERENCE

PACIFIC DIVISION

CENTRAL DIVISION

_____

_____

ATLANTIC DIVISION

METROPOLITAN DIVISION

EASTERN CONFERENCE

_____

_____

The Playoffs

Which two teams will meet in the Stanley Cup Final? Fill in their names below, then circle the team you think will win.

Eastern Conference Winner: _____

Western Conference Winner: _____

YOUR FAVORITE TEAM

Your Team — All Season Long

The standings of hockey teams are listed at NHL.com and on the sports pages of the newspaper all season long. The standings will show you which team is in first place, second place, etc., right down to last place.

Some of the abbreviations you'll become familiar with are: GP for games played; W for wins; L for losses; OT for overtime losses; PTS for points; A for assists; G for goals.

Check the standings on the same day of every month and copy down what they say about your team. By keeping track of your team this way you'll be able to see when it was playing well and when it wasn't.

	GP	W	L	OT	PTS
NOVEMBER 1					
DECEMBER 1					
JANUARY 1					
FEBRUARY 1					
MARCH 1					
APRIL 1					
MAY 1					

Final Standings

At the end of the season print the final record of your team below.

YOUR TEAM	GP	W	L	OT	PTS

Your Favorite Players' Scoring Records

While you're keeping track of your favorite team during the season, you can also follow the progress of your favorite players. Just fill in their point totals on the same day of every month.

player	nov 1	dec 1	jan 1	feb 1	mar 1	apr 1	may 1

Your Favorite Goaltenders' Records

You can keep track of your favorite goaltenders' averages during the season. Just fill in the information below.

GAA is the abbreviation for goals-against average. That's the average number of goals given up by a goaltender during a game over the course of the season.

player	nov 1	dec 1	jan 1	feb 1	mar 1	apr 1	may 1

CRAIG ANDERSON

It only takes one phone call to change a career in pro hockey. The happiest players are the ones who can accept change and make the best of it. Ottawa goalie Craig Anderson is one of those players.

Craig was driving to practice with the Colorado Avalanche on February 18, 2011, when he received a phone call saying that he'd been traded to the Ottawa Senators.

"All I remember is wondering what the call was about, and then being sort of shocked because I wasn't expecting to be traded," he recalls.

"It's a team sport, and you need the guys around you to battle for you; and you need to battle for them."

But Craig looked at the move as a positive one. And it turns out it's been a good one for the veteran netminder. Craig has been the number-one goalie since he arrived in Ottawa, and finished last season with a league-leading 1.69 goals-against average. Based on how he's played since he arrived in Ottawa, Craig will be seriously considered for a place on Team USA for the Sochi Winter Olympics this February.

"My main objective and my goal is just to play for the Ottawa Senators and give them an opportunity to win every night," said Craig last season. "It [a place on Team USA] would be a true honor."

Craig's success hasn't come easily: the Senators are his fourth NHL team and, on a couple of those teams, he spent more time as a back-up goalie than the number-one. Looking back, he can see that those early years on the bench gave him a chance to learn.

"I spent a lot of years backing up some great goaltenders and learning from them and learning how to be a pro and show up every day like the guys you play behind."

Now that Craig has the spotlight, it's quite likely that there are young goalies looking at his positive attitude and work ethic as examples of how to be a true professional.

DID YOU KNOW?
Craig loves Corvettes. For many years he's had a red Corvette painted on one side of his mask. His love of the classic car comes from his dad, who used to race cars when Craig was a kid.

HOCKEY MEMORIES
Craig stole a couple of games for Colorado in the first round of the 2010 playoffs against the heavily favored San Jose Sharks, with the most memorable win being a 51-save 1–0 overtime victory in game three.

GP	W	L	OT	GAA	SO
24	12	9	2	1.69	3

Chicago Blackhawks' 4th choice, 73rd overall, in 2001 NHL Entry Draft
1st NHL Team, Season: Chicago Blackhawks, 2002–2003
Born: May 21, 1981, in Park Ridge, Illinois
Position: Goaltender
Catches: Left
Height: 1.88 m (6'2")
Weight: 82 kg (180 lbs.)

CHICAGO BLACKHAWKS

The last two seasons for Corey Crawford have highlighted what a roller coaster ride being a pro hockey player can be — on a low one minute, the highest high the next. Last year's Stanley Cup high for Corey came right on the heels of a 2011–2012 season where he struggled with his consistency.

"Last year [2011–2012] I felt like I played great hockey at times, but then at other times it was below average," said Corey. "You can't do that and be a number-one guy. You've got to be good every night and give your guys a chance. This year I felt like I had to pay more attention to that."

"Winning the Cup. That's what we play for. That's the ultimate goal."

Even though he wasn't consistent in 2011–2012, Corey still picked up 30 wins for the second season in a row and won eight of his last eleven starts. He also delivered during last year's lockout-shortened season, finishing with a career-best 1.94 goals-against average and winning 19 of the 30 games he played in. Corey shared the William Jennings Trophy for fewest goals given up by a team with teammate Ray Emery. He was a big part of Chicago's season-starting 24-game undefeated streak. During the streak, Corey started 14 of the games, winning his first five starts, before eventually going 11–0–3.

Corey has taken the slow and steady approach to get to his position as one of the NHL's top goalies. He wasn't a 20-year-old phenomenon who stepped into the league and grabbed a number-one job. In fact, he spent most of five full seasons playing in the minors before he managed to crack the Blackhawks roster.

"I was confident [that I'd make it], but there are always negative thoughts that creep in," recalls Corey. "When you're in the minors you have to look past those thoughts and just keep working hard. I just told myself, 'Don't give up, you're not far from your goal.'"

When the Hawks won the Cup in 2010 Corey was in the Chicago system, playing in the minors and dreaming of his chance; last season he was at center stage for the Chicago victory.

DID YOU KNOW?

Corey's goalie coach during his first year of junior hockey was François Allaire, who worked with Hall of Famer Patrick Roy early in his career and is credited with helping Roy perfect the style that made him one of the all-time greats.

HOCKEY MEMORIES

Corey remembers how he felt during his rookie season in the NHL when he was in New York at Madison Square Garden for a game against the Rangers. He realized that he'd finally made it.

2012–2013 STATS

GP	W	L	OT	GAA	SO
30	19	5	5	1.94	3

Chicago Blackhawks' 2nd choice, 52nd overall, in 2003 NHL Entry Draft
1st NHL Team, Season: Chicago Blackhawks, 2010–2011
Born: December 31, 1984, in Montreal, Quebec
Position: Goaltender
Catches: Left
Height: 1.88 m (6'2")
Weight: 94 kg (208 lbs.)

RAPHAEL DIAZ

Raphael Diaz was an experienced player before he ever set a skate on the ice wearing a Montreal Canadiens sweater. Raphael had played eight full seasons in the Swiss National League as well as numerous games for Switzerland at the World Junior Championship, the World Championship and the Olympic Games. Over the last two seasons he's made the transition to the NHL and become one of Montreal's top defensemen.

"He's always been a smart player, but the thing that I really like about him is that he's a competitor. I think people overlook that in him," says teammate and usual defensive partner Josh Gorges. "He's a guy that blocks shots, doesn't mind sticking his nose in there and getting dirty."

Raphael wasn't drafted but rather was signed as a free agent after he'd finished playing for Switzerland at the 2011 World Championship (where he was voted one of the best three players on his team).

Raphael's approach to making the transition from the Swiss League to the NHL was to keep things simple and not get caught up in trying to do too much.

"I just tried to play well defensively and to make the simple, easy pass out of the zone and then try to go and join the rush."

Raphael definitely noticed the difference between European hockey and the NHL.

"You have to see where your teammates are to make the play quickly. Things happen so fast in the NHL," he says. "And, of course, the body contact. They play harder over here."

"To go into the arena, and see how big it is and how loud the crowd is . . . it's an amazing place to play."

Despite missing games with a concussion, Raphael was one of Montreal's key defensemen last season. At the age of 27, he's coming into the prime of his hockey career. Expect even better things from him this season.

DID YOU KNOW?
Raphael's sister, Daniela, is a talented hockey player as well. She played for Switzerland in the 2006 Winter Olympics and the 2007 World Championship.

HOCKEY MEMORIES
Raphael's first NHL game was particularly memorable: it was against Montreal's arch-rivals, the Toronto Maple Leafs.

2012–2013 STATS

GP	G	A	PTS	PIM
23	1	13	14	6

Signed as a free agent by Montreal Canadiens on May 11, 2011
1st NHL Team, Season: Montreal Canadiens, 2011–2012
Born: January 9, 1986, in Baar, Switzerland
Position: Defense
Shoots: Right
Height: 1.8 m (5'11")
Weight: 99 kg (218 lbs.)

PATRIK ELIAS

Patrik Elias is a true NHL superstar. Here are just a few of his many accomplishments with the New Jersey Devils: he's played over 1,000 games with them; he is the all-time franchise leader in goals (375), assists (555), points (930), game-winning goals (78) and most points in a single season (96 points in 2000–2001). He's also the all-time leader in playoff goals (45), assists (80) and points (125). Add to that a couple of Stanley Cup Championships (2000, 2003) and you already have a career worthy of the Hall of Fame. Last season, his fifteenth full NHL season, Patrik showed no signs that he was done with his NHL career. He ended the season as the team's leading scorer with 14 goals, 22 assists and 36 points.

"I've been here my whole career. I've accomplished something here and I am grateful to the Devils for giving me the opportunity to succeed," says Patrik.

Aside from his career with the Devils, Patrik has played in three Olympic Games for the Czech Republic (winning a bronze medal with the 2006 team) and in three World Championships (winning a bronze medal in 1998 and 2011). He is the second-highest-scoring Czech-born player in NHL history — only Jaromir Jagr has scored more points than Patrik.

Aside from being a great hockey player, Patrik is also a keen soccer player.

"It means a lot to me to have played 1,000 games, but even more because they have been with one team."

"It was my first sport," says Patrik. "I started playing when I was eight years old. I played until I was 17 and was playing at a pretty high level. But then I had to choose between hockey and soccer."

Patrik still plays in the off-season and thinks it's a great sport to stay in shape for hockey.

"It's also helped me with my mobility on the ice, as well as agility and quickness. You have to be quick with your feet."

Patrik is lucky enough to be good at two sports — but there can't be much doubt that he chose the right one for a career. He's one of the best.

DID YOU KNOW?
Patrik is the only player in NHL history to have been awarded a penalty shot in overtime twice. Both games were against the New York Islanders, and he missed both chances.

HOCKEY MEMORIES
Patrik remembers his first NHL game and recalls being "anxious, with a lot of energy and nerves. I couldn't wait to get out there, but I didn't do much."

2012–2013 STATS

GP	G	A	PTS	PIM
48	14	22	36	22

New Jersey Devils' 2nd choice, 51st overall, in 1994 NHL Entry Draft
1st NHL Team, Season: New Jersey Devils, 1997–1998
Born: April 13, 1976, in Trebíc, Czechoslovakia (now Czech Republic)
Position: Center
Shoots: Left
Height: 1.85 m (6'1")
Weight: 88 kg (195 lbs.)

TOBIAS ENSTRÖM

Two years ago, when the Atlanta Thrashers left the moderate climate of the southern United States for Winnipeg, it was like getting back a little bit of home for Jets' defenseman Tobias "Toby" Enström. Tobias is from Nordingra, Sweden, and Winnipeg reminds him a little of his hometown.

"It's a smaller place [Nordingra], but it gets pretty cold in the winter and is nice and beautiful in the summer," he says. "But the big thing is that people really love their hockey."

Tobias had hockey fans in Winnipeg pretty excited after last year's shortened season started. At one point he had an eight-game consecutive point-streak (2 goals, 10 assists), was playing just under 26 minutes a game and leading all NHL defensemen in scoring. Then it all came to a crashing halt. Tobias was taken into the boards in the first period of a game against the Pittsburgh Penguins on February 15 and injured his right shoulder. He ended up missing 19 games and had to battle to get back into the lineup. This was, unfortunately, nothing new for Toby. In 2011–2012

he missed 20 games with a broken collarbone — and still managed to finish as the Jets' second-highest scoring blueliner.

Despite his injuries the last couple of seasons, Tobias is still considered one of the top defensemen in the NHL. He's known as a player who is consistent and has what coaches and players call "vision."

> "All of the people around the organization are great. They want to go somewhere with this team, that's one of the big reasons I signed [the contract extension]. They want to win and that's what I want to do."

"He sees the ice well," says Winnipeg coach Claude Noel. "Despite his size he sneaks out of traffic and out of big hits and makes the play. You need good hockey sense to be able to do that."

If the Jets want to continue to build toward playoff success, they'll need Tobias on the ice and healthy this season.

DID YOU KNOW?
Tobias uses an oversize stick — the longest possible under NHL rules. He feels it gives him an advantage as opponents don't always expect him to be able to knock the puck away or intercept a pass.

HOCKEY MEMORIES
Tobias remembers his father, Ulf, coaching him as a young boy, right up until he was 17. He says his dad taught him a lot about the game.

2012–2013 STATS

GP	G	A	PTS	PIM
48	14	22	36	22

Atlanta Thrashers' 8th choice, 239th overall, in 2003 NHL Entry Draft
1st NHL Team, Season: Atlanta Thrashers, 2007–2008
Born: November 5, 1984, in Nordingra, Sweden
Position: Defense
Shoots: Left
Height: 1.78 m (5'10")
Weight: 82 kg (180 lbs.)

TAYLOR HALL

It's been exciting to watch the Edmonton Oilers over the last few seasons. They had some tough years, but it was fun watching talented young players like Jordan Eberle, Ryan Nugent-Hopkins and Taylor Hall improve their game. In 2012–2013 things seemed to move to the next stage of development for the Oilers as they were in the hunt for a playoff spot for the first time in several seasons. One of the key players was Taylor Hall. He led the Oilers in scoring with 16 goals, 34 assists for 50 points. The points total was his second best ever, and would certainly have been a career best had the NHL played a full season. For Taylor, who played with the successful Windsor Spitfires of the Ontario Hockey League, it was a relief to be playing big games down the stretch again.

"I think for us to play in meaningful games where every shift matters, every period matters, is awesome," said Taylor last season. "We're trying to relish it, but also to do something about it."

Taylor and his teammates take their responsibilities as NHL pros seriously — especially in a city like Edmonton where the fans are among the most loyal in hockey. "There's a lot of responsibility being a young guy on a young team," he says. "I can only do so much for the 19 minutes that I'm on the ice . . . that's what you have to focus on. We all have a certain responsibility on and off the ice to lead our team."

"We all love playing in a market where they care; where they come to watch you play and come to watch you win every night."

The Oilers certainly upped their game last season. They were in the chase for their first playoff berth since 2006, but in the end they fell short. While Edmonton fans and players understand that the team has been in a rebuilding phase it's still tough on all involved to be sitting on the sidelines when the puck is dropped for the playoffs.

"It's been a little difficult," admitted Taylor. "I came from a junior team where we did a lot of winning. I think we all understand that it's part of the process, but it can be tough."

Hopefully things will get just a little easier for the Oilers this season.

DID YOU KNOW?

Taylor used Olympic bobsledding methods to cross-train for speed. His dad, Steve, who was a football player in the CFL before he became a nationally ranked bobsledder in Canada, introduced him to it.

HOCKEY MEMORIES

Taylor was awesome in both of his Memorial Cup appearances with the Windsor Spitfires. In 2009 and 2010 they won the title and Taylor was selected as the Most Valuable Player of the tournament — the first and only time that's happened.

GP	G	A	PTS	PIM
45	16	34	50	33

Edmonton Oilers' 1st choice, 1st overall, in 2010 NHL Entry Draft
1st NHL Team, Season: Edmonton Oilers, 2010–2011
Born: November 14, 1991, in Calgary, Alberta
Position: Left Wing
Shoots: Left
Height: 1.85 m (6'1")
Weight: 88 kg (195 lbs.)

NAZEM KADRI

Being a first-round draft pick comes with great expectations. Being a first-round draft pick for a team in a city where hockey is talked about and analyzed every day of the year — a city like Toronto — comes with even greater expectations.

When Nazem Kadri was taken as Toronto's first-round pick in the 2009 NHL Entry Draft, he was being chosen by a team that hadn't had a first-round pick who lived up to expectations in 20 years. There was loads of pressure on both Leafs management, which had selected Nazem, and Nazem himself, who had dreamed about playing for the Leafs.

After he was drafted, Nazem played another season of junior hockey. The next two seasons he bounced up and down between the minors and the NHL — with most of his playing time coming in the minors. There were some who were starting to wonder if Nazem was just going to be another in a long line of first-round picks for Toronto that didn't work out. But he never gave up. He worked hard on his game; in particular he aimed at getting stronger and playing better positional hockey. Last season his hard work and the Leafs' patience started to pay off.

"I definitely feel like I've matured as a player," said Nazem last season. "It also helps a lot when the coach believes in me and has faith in me. It makes you want to work that much harder for him."

"He wants to be a go-to guy in the NHL. I know this from coaching him. He's a tough competitor."
—Dallas Eakins, Kadri's minor league coach

Nazem finished up last season second in team scoring with 18 goals, 26 assists for 44 points, and for the first time in his young career, felt as though he was part of the team and not fighting for a job.

"It's kind of a nice feeling, not having to worry all the time about which game you're going to come up and down."

Nazem is now a key part of the Leafs' game plan; his days in the minors are most definitely finished.

DID YOU KNOW?
Nazem's ethnic background is Lebanese. When he debuted with the Leafs, Nazem became only the third player of Lebanese descent to play in the NHL.

HOCKEY MEMORIES
Nazem earned his first NHL hat trick against the New York Islanders on February 28, 2013, and one of his teammates made sure he got the puck from the third goal. "Dion [Phaneuf] grabbed it for me, so I'm pretty excited to have that."

GP	G	A	PTS	PIM
48	18	26	44	23

Toronto Maple Leafs' 1st choice, 7th overall, in 2009 NHL Entry Draft
1st NHL Team, Season: Toronto Maple Leafs, 2010–2011
Born: October 6, 1990, in London, Ontario
Position: Center
Shoots: Left
Height: 1.83 m (6')
Weight: 85 kg (188 lbs.)

PATRICK KANE

CHICAGO BLACKHAWKS

Patrick Kane's career was so sensational out of the gate that it was almost inevitable that he would hit a a lull. He was named Canadian Major Junior Hockey Rookie of the Year in 2007 and was taken first overall in the NHL Entry Draft, then won the Calder Trophy as NHL Rookie of the Year in 2008. In 2010, Patrick was sipping champagne from the Stanley Cup at the end of only his third NHL season.

"I guess things couldn't have turned out much better," says Patrick.

But his point totals dropped off slightly during his next two seasons. His 66-point total in 2011–2012 was the lowest of his young career.

Patrick was determined to get things back on track last season, and did he ever. He was one of the team's best players during the season and especially during the Hawks' march through the playoffs to the Stanley Cup Championship. Patrick was voted the winner of the Conn Smythe Trophy as the Most Valuable Player in the playoffs.

"I owe it to myself to put the best effort I can forward and prove how good I can play," he said early last season. "With the great start I had to my career, I think that sometimes you feel like it's just going to keep coming to you. But I think I've learned how hard it is and how hard you have to work to get there."

After the NHL lockout ended and teams got back to business, the Blackhawks were the hottest team on ice. At one point early in the shortened season, Chicago set an NHL record by picking up at least one point in 24 consecutive games. Patrick was a big part of the team's success during that streak, as he tallied 27 points. He looked as good as ever, with shots finding the back of the net and passes finding linemates' sticks.

"I don't really ever see myself anywhere else than in Chicago. Great city, great organization and we have a great team, too."

"If there was one word I had to use to describe myself as a player, I guess it would be 'playmaker.' Getting the puck and making plays with it, scoring goals, getting pucks to the net. That's me, I think."

Chicago fans might choose the word "superstar" instead.

DID YOU KNOW?
Patrick first wore number 88 when he was with the London Knights in the Ontario Hockey League. He chose the number because it has the last two digits of his birth year — 1988.

HOCKEY MEMORIES
It's pretty tough to top scoring the Stanley Cup-winning goal in overtime, as Patrick did on June 9, 2010. "It's something you dream about . . . "

2012–2013 STATS

GP	G	A	PTS	PIM
47	23	32	55	8

Chicago Blackhawks' 1st choice, 1st overall, in 2007 NHL Entry Draft
1st NHL Team, Season: Chicago Blackhawks, 2007–2008
Born: November 19, 1988, in Buffalo, New York
Position: Right Wing
Shoots: Left
Height: 1.8 m (5'11")
Weight: 82 kg (181 lbs.)

GABRIEL LANDESKOG

It's safe to say that last season couldn't have started soon enough for Colorado superstar Gabriel Landeskog. After all, the outstanding young Swedish-born player was coming off a sensational rookie season where he was named the Calder Trophy winner as NHL Rookie of the Year.

Gabriel led his team in goal scoring (22) during his rookie season and was the youngest player in franchise history to do so. A few months later he was named the youngest captain in NHL history. Landeskog was 19 years, 286 days old when the Avalanche awarded him the C — 11 days younger than Sidney Crosby was when he was named captain of the Pittsburgh Penguins.

"I'm so humbled and grateful for this opportunity, and what an honor to follow in the footsteps of past captains for the Avs," said Gabriel. "I couldn't be more excited."

Back in the 2010–2011 season you would have heard lots of talk about Gabriel's play in the Ontario Hockey League with the Kitchener Rangers. Most scouts felt that he would be able to step right into the NHL. His play was strong in both ends of the rink and he was, even at the age of 18, recognized as someone who would be a leader (he was named captain of Kitchener when he was 17 years old).

Last year was a tougher one for Gabriel, though. He took a hit to the head during a game in late January and struggled with the effects of a concussion. He didn't play again until late February.

"I do see myself as a skill player, but it still comes down to hard work, and I think being gritty and kind of in-your-face is what I want to do."

"It was very frustrating. You come back after your first season, then the lockout and you just want to prove yourself again. I just wanted to play my game, do my thing, and then I get hurt."

Gabriel did manage to contribute 9 goals, 8 assists for 17 points during a frustrating season for the Avs, but he's confident this season will bring better things for both him and his teammates.

DID YOU KNOW?
Gabriel has a few game-day superstitions: Pregame meal should be salmon and, when he gets geared up, it's always right side first.

HOCKEY MEMORIES
Gabriel's first NHL goal made him the youngest Swedish-born player ever to score in the NHL.

2012–2013 STATS

GP	G	A	PTS	PIM
36	9	8	17	22

Colorado Avalanche's 1st choice, 2nd overall, in 2011 NHL Entry Draft
1st NHL Team, Season: Colorado Avalanche, 2011–2012
Born: November 23, 1992, in Stockholm, Sweden
Position: Left Wing
Shoots: Left
Height: 1.85 m (6'1")
Weight: 93 kg (204 lbs.)

EVGENI MALKIN

PITTSBURGH PENGUINS

It's obvious that Evgeni "Geno" Malkin is a superstar. In his seven seasons with the Pittsburgh Penguins, he's won the Stanley Cup, the Hart Trophy as the Most Valuable Player, the Ted Lindsay Award (outstanding player as voted by other NHL players), the Art Ross Trophy (scoring champion), the Conn Smythe Trophy (Most Valuable Player of the playoffs) and the Calder Trophy (Rookie of the Year).

What's even more impressive is that he's had to adjust to playing in the best hockey league in the world on top of learning to live in a very different world from the one he grew up in, in Magnitorgorsk, Russia. Evgeni couldn't speak a word of English when he arrived in Pittsburgh. Imagine living in a place where you couldn't understand what was being said. Now imagine having to deal with people who want to interview you and ask you about playing in the NHL.

"It took me some time, but [learning to speak] English became a higher priority for me, and I became more confident about knowing what to say," Evgeni told a Russian-language newspaper. "You're nervous when you can't say what you want, and you get tense."

Evgeni enjoyed his time back in Russia at the start of last season. He played the first part of the season, during the lockout, with his hometown team in Magnitogorsk.

"I had a big injury and came back and played well. We had a great line, but we didn't win the Stanley Cup. I want to win the Stanley Cup again. It's always my target."

"I enjoyed my time in Magnitogorsk, but I missed Pittsburgh and the people and my friends," Evgeni said. "I worked hard every day in practices and games. I wanted to be ready."

But Geno seemed to have trouble finding his groove as he dealt with a concussion and a couple of other injuries that restricted him to 31 games. However, he turned it on in the Pens' playoff run with 16 points in 15 games — a positive sign heading into this season.

DID YOU KNOW?
Although almost everyone spells Evgeni's nickname as "Geno," he has it spelled on his custom-made sticks as "Gino."

HOCKEY MEMORIES
Evgeni called winning the scoring title, the Hart Trophy and the Ted Lindsay Award in 2012 "a special day . . . one of the best days of my life."

2012–2013 STATS

GP	G	A	PTS	PIM
31	9	24	33	36

Pittsburgh Penguins' 1st choice, 2nd overall, in 2004 NHL Entry Draft

1st NHL Team, Season: Pittsburgh Penguins, 2006–2007

Born: July 31, 1986, in Magnitogorsk, Russia

Position: Center

Shoots: Left

Height: 1.9 m (6'3")

Weight: 96 kg (212 lbs.)

BRAD MARCHAND

Brad Marchand is always up for a fight. That doesn't always have to mean the "drop the gloves" kind of fight, but rather playing hard and battling an opponent for every inch of ice, every loose puck, from start to finish in every game. He reminds many of former NHL superstar Theo Fleury, who played a similar style and enjoyed a career that spanned over 1,000 NHL games. Like Fleury, Brad has always had to listen to others saying he was "too small to play in the NHL" and would never make it. But to underestimate Brad's determination and his strength is a mistake.

"I was always taught to be gritty and work hard," says Brad. "That's something that's come through our family. It's a good trait and it's gotten me to where I am."

The grittiness is part of Brad's game, but he wouldn't be in the NHL if he couldn't score. His scoring ability is what scouts noticed when he was playing junior hockey in the Quebec Major Junior Hockey League with the Moncton Wildcats, Val d'Or Foreurs and Halifax Mooseheads. In particular, scouts were impressed with Brad's play in the big games. During the 2007 playoffs with Val d'Or, Brad led all playoff scorers with 40 points in 20 games. He also played in two World Junior Championship tournaments with Canada — helping win gold in both 2007 and 2008.

> "He seems to have a knack to come up with some timely goals or hits or he just generates energy and chances with his skating. He hustles and gives his all on every shift."
> — Boston teammate Patrice Bergeron

Brad's determination to play hard in the important games first became obvious during the Bruins' 2011 Stanley Cup run. Brad scored 11 goals during that playoff year — more than any other rookie in Bruins playoff history. In the 2011 Final, Brad picked up 7 points in 7 games and scored 2 goals in the Cup-clinching Game Seven against Vancouver. Although the Bruins lost in the Final last season, Brad was still one of their top post-season players with his gritty style — a style Bruins fans have come to love and expect from number 63.

DID YOU KNOW?

Brad is one of only 11 players in NHL history to have scored 2 or more goals in a Game 7 in the Stanley Cup Final.

HOCKEY MEMORIES

After winning the Stanley Cup, Brad spent his day with the Cup in Halifax, Nova Scotia, and started the day off by eating a big bowl of cereal out of it.

2012–2013 STATS

GP	G	A	PTS	PIM
45	18	18	36	27

Boston Bruins' 4th choice, 71st overall, in 2006 NHL Entry Draft
1st NHL Team, Season: Boston Bruins, 2009–2010
Born: May 11, 1988, in Halifax, Nova Scotia
Position: Left Wing
Shoots: Left
Height: 1.75 m (5'9")
Weight: 83 kg (183 lbs.)

CAREY PRICE

Playing goal for any NHL team is an extremely demanding job, but when you're the number-one goalie for the Montreal Canadiens, the job can be like no other. The Canadiens have won 24 Stanley Cup Championships — more than any other NHL team. Fifty-three players who have donned the Montreal *bleu, blanc et rouge* are members of the Hockey Hall of Fame. The Canadiens play in a city where their fans and the media expect winners. When the team is doing well, the players are treated like heroes. However, when the team struggles, the criticism can be very intense.

"It's easy to get wrapped up in what's in the media, what's being said or what's being written," says Carey. "But, at the end of the day, you just have to believe in yourself."

Carey has responded well to the demands of being the number-one goalie in Montreal, consistently ranking among the top of the NHL goaltending stats in wins and games played. Last season he played in 39 of Montreal's 48 games, finishing with 21 wins, the seventh best total in the league. He also hit the milestone of 300 career games with the Habs.

"Well, sometimes it feels like it's been 600 games," said Carey when asked about the milestone after game 300.

> "Here, everything is magnified tenfold. Your slumps are magnified, your streaks are magnified. Everything is extreme highs and lows and that's something you have to manage."

As you'd expect with any athlete over time — he's now played six seasons with the Canadiens — Carey has continued to develop his game. However, he has consistently maintained a low-key mental approach. He appears not to get too excited during the winning streaks and doesn't show any signs of panic when he occasionally struggles. Unfortunately, both he and the team struggled during last year's first-round playoff exit to Ottawa. Carey gave up 13 goals in four games. He will undoubtedly battle back this season, well aware of the fact that great Montreal goalies are judged not by their wins, but by Stanley Cups. In Montreal, those expectations come with the job.

DID YOU KNOW?

Sometimes during the off-season Carey participates in local rodeos in a two-man team in the Team Calf Roping Event. He says it helps him relax.

HOCKEY MEMORIES

Carey was a star for Canada at the 2007 World Junior Hockey Championship in Sweden. He led Canada to a gold medal and was named Best Goaltender and Most Valuable Player of the tournament.

DANIEL SEDIN

In June 2014, it will be 15 years since the Vancouver Canucks and their general manager at the time, Brian Burke, pulled off a series of dramatic draft day deals to make sure that the Canucks would be able to select two young talents from Sweden: Daniel and Henrik Sedin. At the time, Burke said the Sedins "were character kids with a great work ethic and we know they'll get better." How right he was.

Both players are as renowned for their hard work during off-ice training sessions as they are for their great touch with the puck.

Daniel's attention to fitness has paid off. Both Daniel and Henrik have suited up for over 900 games each in a Canucks sweater; Daniel is second in all-time franchise scoring with 758 points, his brother Henrik is the all-time leader with 792. The two have spent most of their careers playing together on the same line and won back-to-back NHL scoring titles (Henrik in 2009–2010 and Daniel in 2010–2011).

"It's spectacular to watch those two get going," says Canucks associate coach Rick Bowness. "They're world-class elite players,

and they find a way to get it done."

Aside from Daniel's major role with the Canucks, he'll be a major part of Sweden's team for the Sochi Winter Olympics later this season. He never tires of putting on the sweater for his country.

"The Stanley Cup has to be the toughest trophy to win. You play 82 games just to get into the playoffs; after that you might play another 28 games to win it."

"In Sweden the goal growing up is playing for the national team and of course the Olympics. When you get a chance to put that jersey on, it's a big deal."

After Vancouver's first-round playoff exit last season, Daniel and Henrik jumped at the chance to play for Sweden at the World Championship in Stockholm. They helped Sweden win the gold medal. Daniel had 6 points in the four games he played, while Henrik chipped in with 9 points. Great efforts from both players — something Brian Burke was sure he could expect all those years ago.

DID YOU KNOW?
Both Sedins were centermen when they played the game as kids. However, after they turned 12, the coach on a new team decided that he wanted them to play on the same line so Daniel switched to the wing, while Henrik remained a center.

HOCKEY MEMORIES
Daniel was part of Sweden's Olympic gold-medal-winning team in 2006 in Turin, Italy. He once said that the gold medal he received had a proud place in his daughter's toy box!

2012–2013 STATS

GP	G	A	PTS	PIM
47	12	28	40	18

Vancouver Canucks' 1st choice, 2nd overall, in 1999 NHL Entry Draft
1st NHL Team, Season: Vancouver Canucks, 2000–2001
Born: September 26, 1980, in Ornskoldsvik, Sweden
Position: Left Wing
Shoots: Left
Height: 1.85 m (6'1")
Weight: 85 kg (187 lbs.)

STEVEN STAMKOS

There was nothing spectacular about Steven Stamkos's 200th NHL career goal last season — it was an empty net goal against the Philadelphia Flyers on March 18, 2013. Still, the goal was a special one: it made him the fourth-youngest player to hit the 200-goal mark, behind Wayne Gretzky, Mario Lemieux and Dale Hawerchuk. To top it off, Steven was once again among the top goal scorers in the league — finishing with 29, second to Alex Ovechkin's top total of 32.

When you ask other players around the league about Steven, there is plenty of talk about "his trademark one-timer" and how he gets himself open and "can score from almost anywhere." But teammates and coaches are also quick to point out that Steven is a good two-way player — meaning that he worries about his defensive responsibilities and not just scoring goals.

"I think my game has evolved the last couple of years," he says. "When you're a centerman, and with the puck possession game that's played today, you want to be that guy that can be on the ice in all situations. Whether you need a goal or whether you're protecting a one-goal lead."

". . . to me, the guy I think about right away is Steven Stamkos. He's the best natural goal scorer in the league."
—Sidney Crosby, on his rival for MVP

There are other parts of Steven's game that have changed. Little things, like where he sets up or the angle he shoots from — things most people would barely notice. With advance scouting and video analysis and almost every game televised, the best defensive players and goalies soon figure out what to expect. So the best players will always try to make subtle tweaks to their game to keep opponents guessing.

"You pretty much have to reinvent your game every year," laughs Steven.

The adjustments and hard work seem to work fine. There are still many years to go but, right now, Steven is on pace to be one of the finest goal scorers of his era.

DID YOU KNOW?
Steven has scored 185 goals in the last four seasons — more than any other player in the NHL.

HOCKEY MEMORIES
"I remember getting out on the frozen ponds in the winter, and it was something I fell in love with early."

2012–2013 STATS

GP	G	A	PTS	PIM
48	29	28	57	32

Tampa Bay Lightning's 1st choice, 1st overall, in 2008 NHL Entry Draft
1st NHL Team, Season: Tampa Bay Lightning, 2008–2009
Born: February 7, 1990, in Markham, Ontario
Position: Center
Shoots: Right
Height: 1.85 m (6'1")
Weight: 85 kg (188 lbs.)

THOMAS VANEK

It takes a lot to make it to the NHL, and one of the most important things that an aspiring young player requires is determination. From the time he was young, Buffalo superstar Thomas Vanek was determined that one day he'd suit up for an NHL team.

Thomas was born and raised in Austria. Although he learned to play hockey there, he realized that he could develop into a better player by heading to North America. So, at the age of 14, Thomas set off for Canada where he played a season of AAA hockey before heading to the United States Hockey League — the top junior league in the U.S. — where he played three seasons with the Sioux Falls Stampede. Thomas kept pushing towards his dream, and the next stop was the University of Minnesota where he starred with the Golden Gophers before being drafted by the Buffalo Sabres in the first round of the 2003 NHL Entry Draft. Thomas was close to achieving his goal of playing in the NHL. He played another season of university hockey, followed by a season in the American Hockey League, before finally stepping on to the ice as an NHL player on October 5, 2005.

Ask hockey people about the secret to Vanek's success, and the answer you will always receive is that Thomas possesses "a natural offensive touch."

"He's one of those skilled guys who can score on the rush, can score from the inside . . . he finds the puck and the puck finds him," says Buffalo assistant coach James Patrick.

"Ever since I could walk, I was at the rink . . . The appeal of the game was bigger to me than any of the other popular sports in Austria."

Last season Thomas enjoyed his best NHL season yet. He started with an eight-game point scoring streak and never looked back, ending the season with a team-leading 20 goals, 21 assists for 41 points.

Thomas was determined to make it to the NHL, and he has. He's also determined to win a Stanley Cup. One dream down and one big one to go.

DID YOU KNOW?
Thomas was the first European-born player ever to play for the University of Minnesota Golden Gophers. He was named the team's Most Valuable Player during his first season there.

HOCKEY MEMORIES
During his rookie season with the Golden Gophers, Thomas helped lead the team to the title at the famous Frozen Four Tournament. He scored the game-winning goal in both the semi-final game and the championship game.

2012–2013 STATS

GP	G	A	PTS	PIM
38	20	21	41	20

Buffalo Sabres' 1st choice, 5th overall, in 2003 NHL Entry Draft
1st NHL Team, Season: Buffalo Sabres, 2005–2006
Born: January 19, 1984, in Vienna, Austria
Position: Left Wing
Shoots: Right
Height: 1.88 m (6'2")
Weight: 93 kg (205 lbs.)

HENRIK ZETTERBERG

The 2012–2013 NHL season may have started late, but it was a memorable beginning for Detroit superstar Henrik Zetterberg. On January 15, 2013, he was named Detroit's thirty-sixth captain. He took the captain's torch from fellow Swede Nicklas Lidstrom.

"This is something you dream about," said Henrik at the time. "The first person I called to tell was my father back in Sweden. He taught me how to play and I learned to love the game from him."

It has been 10 seasons now since Henrik arrived in Detroit as a late draft pick and, in the minds of some, a bit of a question mark. Some felt he was a bit on the small side for an NHL forward and perhaps not a good enough skater. Did those critics ever turn out to be wrong. Heading into his eleventh season, Henrik is considered to be the finest two-way player in the game. Just ask one of the greatest players of them all, Wayne Gretzky.

"My favorite player over the last 10 years has been Zetterberg. I think Zetterberg is the best player in the game [at his age]. He's been so physically beat up from the Stanley Cup playoffs, Olympics, all that goes with that, but he's just very special," said Gretzky.

"The difference between good players and great players often isn't skill level, it's how determined they are and what they bring. The competitive guy wants to be the best."
—Detroit coach Mike Babcock on Zetterberg's attitude

There are so many things that have contributed to Henrik's success. One of the most important was something he didn't like at the time — how much smaller he was than his friends in his early teens.

"I remember that all of my friends started to get bigger and I didn't," he says. "But I think that made me really work on my skills and finding other ways to get things done. I gradually got a little bigger, but I think I had better skills because of the way things turned out."

Two great attributes to have for an NHL player: positive attitude and determination. That's why he's one of the best.

DID YOU KNOW?

Henrik was so unsure of being drafted by an NHL team that he wasn't even at the draft when he was taken in the 7th round in 1999. He was on holiday in Cyprus with some friends and got the news when a Swedish scout phoned him.

HOCKEY MEMORIES

"The Red Wings brought me over to watch the team play during the 2002 playoffs, and I remember walking into the locker room for the first time and seeing the names: Chelios, Robitaille, Larionov, Fedorov, and thinking 'Wow.' I'll always remember that."

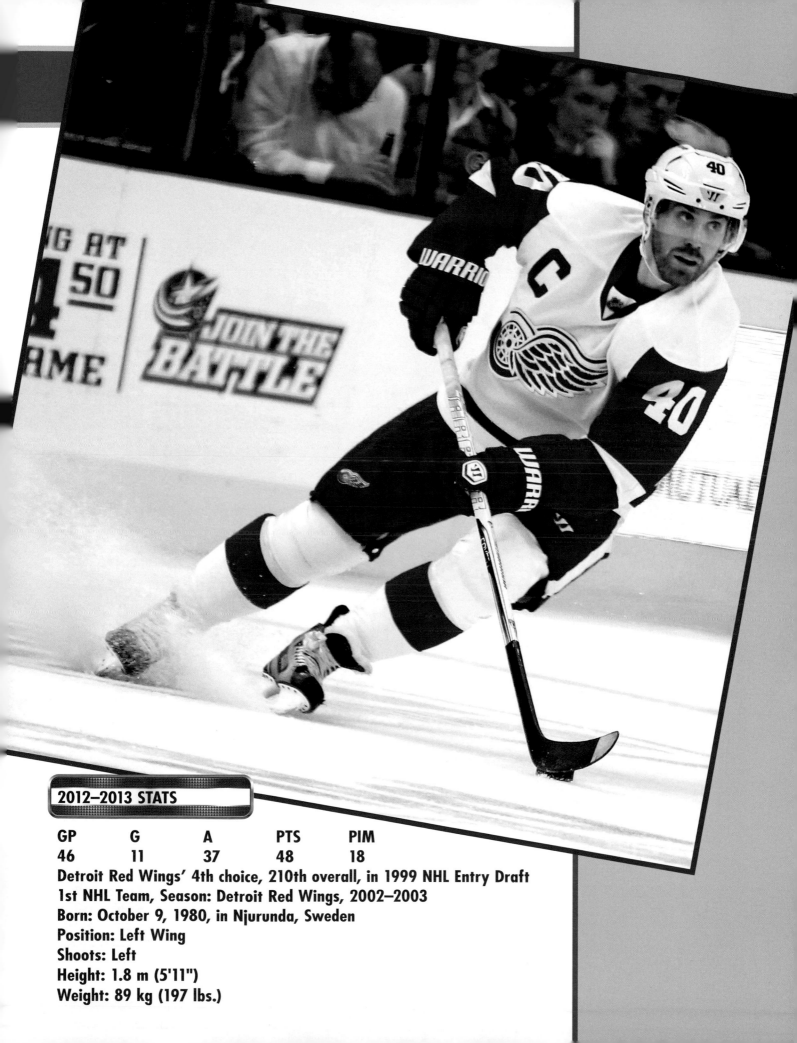

2012–2013 STATS

GP	G	A	PTS	PIM
46	11	37	48	18

Detroit Red Wings' 4th choice, 210th overall, in 1999 NHL Entry Draft
1st NHL Team, Season: Detroit Red Wings, 2002–2003
Born: October 9, 1980, in Njurunda, Sweden
Position: Left Wing
Shoots: Left
Height: 1.8 m (5'11")
Weight: 89 kg (197 lbs.)

REFEREE SIGNALS

Do you know what is happening when the referee stops play and makes a penalty call? If you don't, then you're missing an important part of the game. The referee can call different penalties that result in anything from playing a man short for two minutes to having a player kicked out of the game.

Here are some of the most common referee signals. Now you'll know what penalties are being called against your team.

Boarding
Checking an opponent into the boards in a violent way.

Charging
Checking an opponent in a violent way as a result of skating or charging at him.

Cross-checking
Striking an opponent with the stick, while both hands are on the stick and both arms are extended.

Elbowing
Checking an opponent with an elbow.

High-sticking
Striking an opponent with the stick, which is held above shoulder height.

Holding
Holding back an opponent with the hands or arms.

Hooking
Using the blade of the stick to hold back an opponent.

Icing
Shooting the puck across the opposing team's goal line from one's own side of the rink. Called only if the opposing player touches the puck first.

Interference
Holding back an opponent who does not have the puck in play.

Kneeing
Using a knee to hold back an opponent.

Misconduct
A ten-minute penalty — the longest type called. Usually for abuse of an official.

Roughing
Shoving or striking an opponent.

REFEREE SIGNALS

Slashing
Using the stick to strike an opponent.

Spearing
Poking an opponent with the blade of the stick.

Slow whistle
The official waits to blow his whistle because of a delayed offside or delayed penalty call. Done while the opposing team has control of the puck.

Tripping
Tripping an opponent with the stick, a hand or a foot.

Unsportsmanlike conduct
Showing poor sportsmanship toward an opponent. For example: biting, pulling hair, etc.

Wash-out
Goal not allowed.

FINAL TEAM STANDINGS 2012-2013

EASTERN CONFERENCE

Atlantic Division

Team	GP	W	L	OT	PTS
PITTSBURGH	48	36	12	0	72
NY RANGERS	48	26	18	4	56
NY ISLANDERS	48	24	17	7	55
PHILADELPHIA	48	23	22	3	49
NEW JERSEY	48	19	19	10	48

Northeast Division

Team	GP	W	L	OT	PTS
MONTREAL	48	29	14	5	63
BOSTON	48	28	14	6	62
TORONTO	48	26	17	5	57
OTTAWA	48	25	17	6	56
BUFFALO	48	21	21	6	48

Southeast Division

Team	GP	W	L	OT	PTS
WASHINGTON	48	27	18	3	57
WINNIPEG	48	24	21	3	51
CAROLINA	48	19	25	4	42
TAMPA BAY	48	18	26	4	40
FLORIDA	48	15	27	6	36

WESTERN CONFERENCE

Central Division

Team	GP	W	L	OT	PTS
CHICAGO	48	36	7	5	77
ST. LOUIS	48	29	17	2	60
DETROIT	48	24	16	8	56
COLUMBUS	48	24	17	7	55
NASHVILLE	48	16	23	9	41

Northwest Division

Team	GP	W	L	OT	PTS
VANCOUVER	48	26	15	7	59
MINNESOTA	48	26	19	3	55
EDMONTON	48	19	22	7	45
CALGARY	48	19	25	4	42
COLORADO	48	16	25	7	39

Pacific Division

Team	GP	W	L	OT	PTS
ANAHEIM	48	30	12	6	66
LOS ANGELES	48	27	16	5	59
SAN JOSE	48	25	16	7	57
PHOENIX	48	21	18	9	51
DALLAS	48	22	22	4	48

GP = Games played; W = Wins; L = Losses; OT = Overtime; PTS = Points

Top Ten Points Leaders 2012-2013

PLAYER	TEAM	GP	G	A	P	S	S%
1 MARTIN ST LOUIS	TAMPA BAY	48	17	43	60	112	15.2
2 STEVEN STAMKOS	TAMPA BAY	48	29	28	57	157	18.5
3 ALEX OVECHKIN	WASHINGTON	48	32	24	56	220	14.5
4 SIDNEY CROSBY	PITTSBURGH	36	15	41	56	124	12.1
5 PATRICK KANE	CHICAGO	47	23	32	55	38	16.7
6 ERIC STAAL	CAROLINA	48	18	35	53	152	11.8
7 CHRIS KUNITZ	PITTSBURGH	48	22	30	52	113	19.5
8 PHIL KESSEL	TORONTO	48	20	32	52	161	12.4
9 TAYLOR HALL	EDMONTON	45	16	34	50	154	10.4
10 PAVEL DATSYUK	DETROIT	47	15	34	49	107	14.0

GP = Games played; G = Goals; A = Assists; P = Points;
S = Shots; S% = Percentage

Top Ten Goalies — Total Wins 2012-2013

PLAYER	TEAM	GP	W	L	OT	SA%	GA	GAA
1 HENRIK LUNDQVIST	NY RANGERS	43	24	16	3	.926	88	2.05
2 ANTTI NIEMI	SAN JOSE	43	24	12	6	.924	93	2.16
3 NIKLAS BACKSTROM	MINNESOTA	42	24	15	3	.909	98	2.48
4 MARC-ANDRE FLEURY	PITTSBURGH	33	23	8	0	.916	74	2.39
5 EVGENI NABOKOV	NY ISLANDERS	41	23	11	7	.910	103	2.50
6 BRADEN HOLTBY	WASHINGTON	36	23	12	1	.920	90	2.58
7 SERGEI BOBROVSKY	COLUMBUS	38	21	11	6	.932	74	2.00
8 JIMMY HOWARD	DETROIT	42	21	13	7	.923	87	2.13
9 CAREY PRICE	MONTREAL	39	21	13	4	.905	97	2.59
10 ONDREJ PAVELEC	WINNIPEG	44	21	20	3	.905	119	2.80

GP = Games played; W = Wins; L = Losses; OT = Overtime and/or Shut-Out Losses;
SA% = Save percentage; GA = Goals Against; GAA = Goals-Against Average

END-OF-SEASON STATS

Countdown to the Cup 2013–2014

EASTERN CONFERENCE

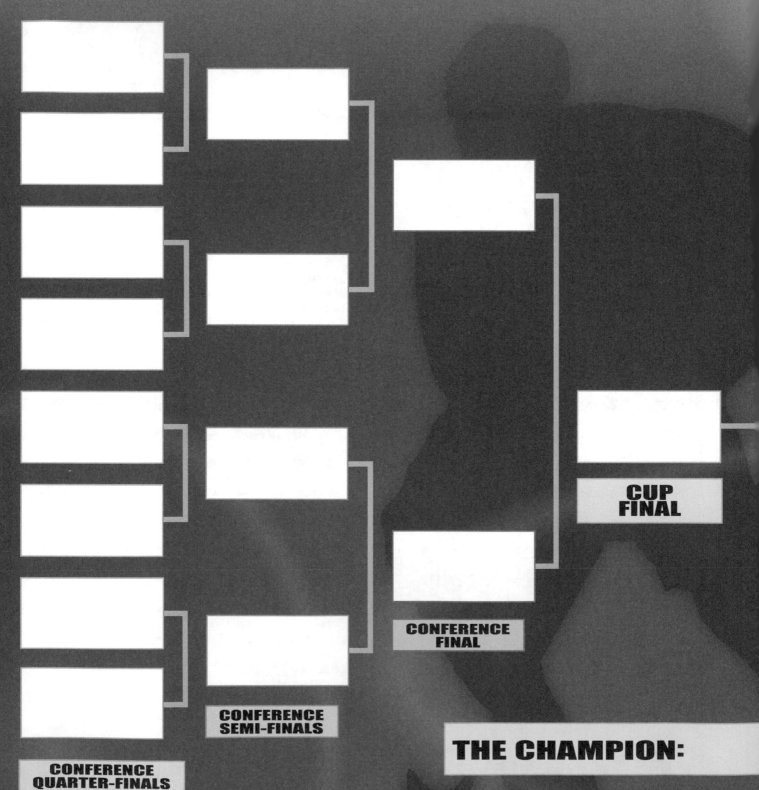

**CONFERENCE
QUARTER-FINALS**

**CONFERENCE
SEMI-FINALS**

**CONFERENCE
FINAL**

**CUP
FINAL**

THE CHAMPION:

WESTERN CONFERENCE

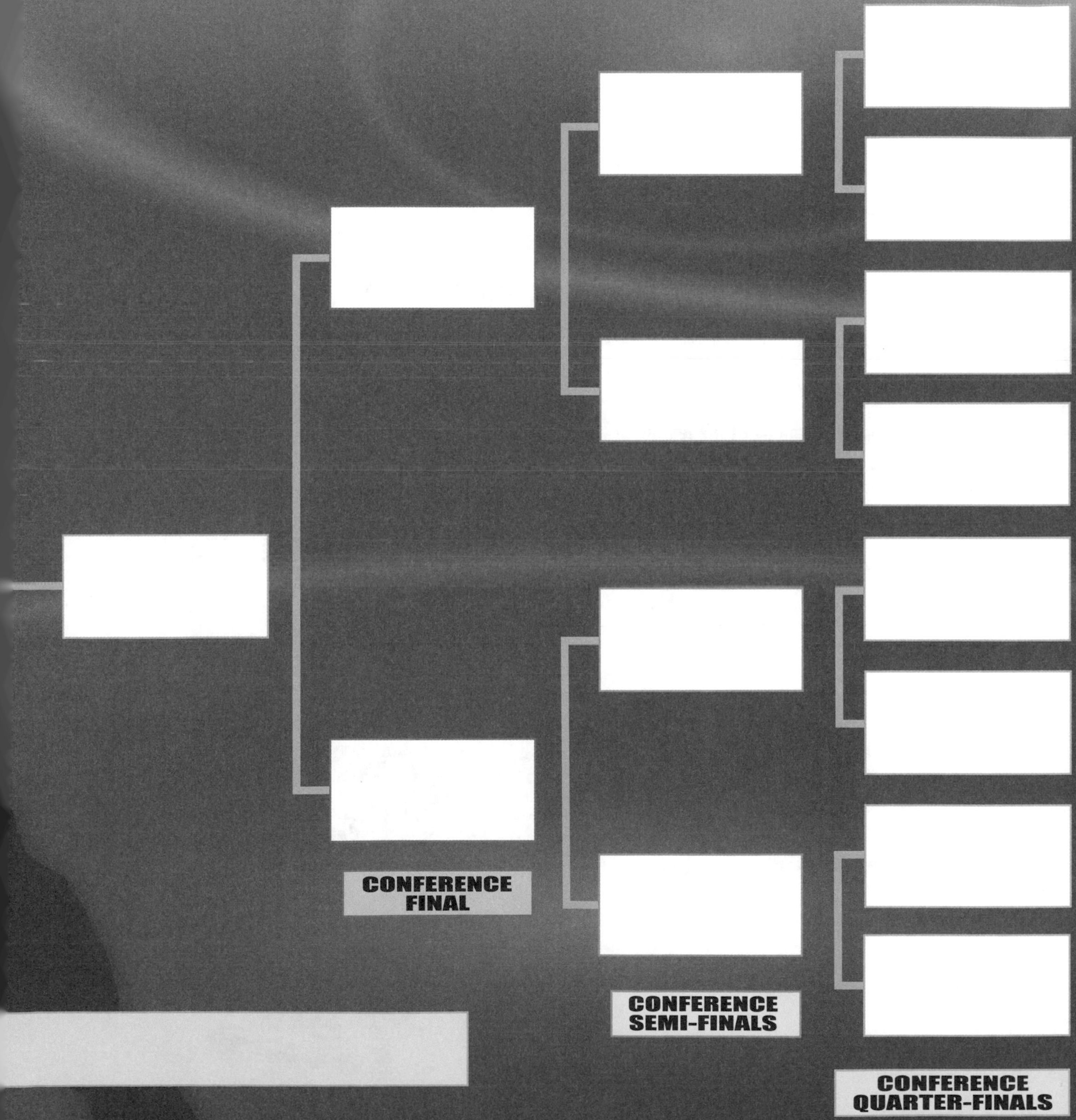

CONFERENCE FINAL

CONFERENCE SEMI-FINALS

CONFERENCE QUARTER-FINALS

NHL AWARDS

Here are some of the major NHL awards for individual players. Fill in your selection for each award and then fill in the name of the actual winner of the trophy.

HART MEMORIAL TROPHY

Awarded to the player judged to be the most valuable to his team. Selected by the Professional Hockey Writers Association.

2013 winner: **Alexander Ovechkin**

Your choice for 2014: _____

The winner: _____

ART ROSS TROPHY

Awarded to the player who leads the league in scoring points at the end of the regular season.

2013 winner: **Martin St. Louis**

Your choice for 2014: _____

The winner: _____

CALDER MEMORIAL TROPHY

Awarded to the player selected as the most proficient in his first year of competition in the NHL. Selected by the Professional Hockey Writers Association.

2013 winner: **Jonathan Huberdeau**

Your choice for 2014: _____

The winner: _____

JAMES NORRIS TROPHY

Awarded to the defense player who demonstrates throughout his season the greatest all-round ability. Selected by the Professional Hockey Writers Association.

2013 winner: **P.K. Subban**

Your choice for 2014: _____

The winner: _____

VEZINA TROPHY

Awarded to the goalkeeper judged to be the best. Selected by the NHL general managers.

2013 winner: **Sergei Bobrovsky**

Your choice for 2014: _____

The winner: _____

MAURICE RICHARD TROPHY

Awarded to the player who scores the highest number of regular-season goals.

2013 winner: **Alexander Ovechkin**

Your choice for 2014: _____

The winner: _____

WILLIAM M. JENNINGS TROPHY

Awarded to the goalkeeper(s) who played a minimum of 25 games for the team with the fewest goals scored against it.

2013 winners: **Corey Crawford and Ray Emery**

Your choice for 2014: _____

The winner: _____

LADY BYNG MEMORIAL TROPHY

Awarded to the player judged to have exhibited the best sportsmanship combined with a high standard of playing ability. Selected by the Professional Hockey Writers Association.

2013 winner: **Martin St. Louis**

Your choice for 2014: _____

The winner: _____

FRANK J. SELKE TROPHY

Awarded to the forward who best excels in the defensive aspects of the game. Selected by the Professional Hockey Writers Association.

2013 winner: **Jonathan Toews**

Your choice for 2014: _____

The winner: _____

CONN SMYTHE TROPHY

Awarded to the player most valuable to his team in the Stanley Cup Playoffs. Selected by the Professional Hockey Writers Association.

2013 winner: **Patrick Kane**

Your choice for 2014: _____

The winner: _____

BILL MASTERTON MEMORIAL TROPHY

Awarded to the player who best exemplifies the qualitites of perseverance, sportsmanship and dedication to hockey. Selected by the Professional Hockey Writers Association.

2013 winner: **Josh Harding**

Your choice for 2014: _____

The winner: _____

For more than 12 years of smiles, laughs and licks —
to the memory of my oldie golden retriever, London.
—P.R.

AUTHOR'S ACKNOWLEDGEMENTS: Thanks to NHL.com,
NHLPA.com, the Hockey Hall of Fame, and the personal websites of
players profiled as well as IIHF.com, hockeydb.com and eliteprospects.com
for additional sources of information.

Author photo: Andre Ringuette/HHOF-IIHF Images

Illustrations by Bill Dickson

Photo credits:
Anderson: Patrick McDermott/NHLI via Getty Images
Crawford: Bill Smith/NHLI via Getty Images
Crosby: G Fiume/Getty Images
Diaz: Francois Lacasse/NHLI via Getty Images
Elias: Elsa/Getty Images
Enstrom: Lance Thomson/NHLI via Getty Images
Hall: Thearon W. Henderson/Getty Images
Kadri: Jana Chytilova/Freestyle/Getty Images
Kane: Frederick Breedon/via Getty Images
Landeskog: Noah Graham/NHLI via Getty Images
Malkin: Gregory Shamus/NHLI via Getty Images
Marchand: Steve Babineau/NHLI via Getty Images
Price: Richard Wolowicz/Getty Images
Sedin: Jeff Vinnick/NHLI via Getty Images
Stamkos: Scott Audette/NHLI via Getty Images
Vanek: Jim McIsaac/Getty Images
Zetterberg: Kirk Irwin/Getty Images

ISBN 978-1-4431-2878-0 (U.S. Edition)
ISBN 978-1-4431-2489-8 (Canadian Edition)
Copyright © 2013 by Scholastic Canada Ltd.

6 5 4 3 2 1   Printed in Canada 118   13 14 15 16